courageous
conversations

ALSO BY ERIN MICHELLE

show me your scars

courageous conversations

erin michelle

illustrations by emily joy johnson

Copyright © 2022 by Erin Michelle Murray

All rights reserved.

ISBN: 9781778090813

CONTENT WARNING

this book contains themes pertaining to mental illness

depression, anxiety, suicide, addiction, and abuse are all discussed

read gently and feel vastly but put your wellbeing first

with love,
erin michelle

MENTAL HEALTH RESOURCES

Canadian Mental Health Association: https://cmha.ca/
Mental Health America: https://mhanational.org/
This Is My Brave: https://thisismybrave.org/

DEDICATION

to Tori, for every courageous conversation you encouraged me to have and every day you have continued to make this world better for those who need it most

FOREWORD

this isn't a happy story, yet it is not unpleasant either
beauty and pain do not negate one another
this book absolutely shattered me and healed me
simultaneously
it is the rawness of mental illness
the journey to acceptance of a pain I may never be rid of
it is real and agonizing and courageous
it is the immensity of love, identity, addiction,
hopelessness, anguish, and acceptance
it is my story

CONTENTS

Journey   i

Exhaustion   1

Lover   15

Angst   43

Illuminations   67

Despondent   87

Reflections   111

JOURNEY

craft something beautiful, they said
create words that paint pictures
and rumination that inspires compositions
let your pain create beauty
give to the world that which has scored you deeply
share your vulnerable moments
the days you thought you would cease to exist
hours you marched with weights on your chest
the minutes you hid in dark corners of your mind
and the seconds so painful they took years to pass
so here are my words
let me cradle your heart with sentences
thereafter, let me shatter it with prose
let each word hit its mark
as I hunt for your sentiment
and craft something beautiful
out of that which has nearly broken me

EXHAUSTION

erin michelle

exhaustion has become the companion
I did not want
a toxic lover who holds me in the night
yet strikes with words and fists during day
leaving bruises under eyes
and a shake in my hands

he caresses my face, streaking mascara
and knots his hands in my hair
leaving it a mess of tangles
indicative of the web of lies he weaves at night
while he whispers me to a restless sleep
that will do nothing to sooth the torment of day

please let me go

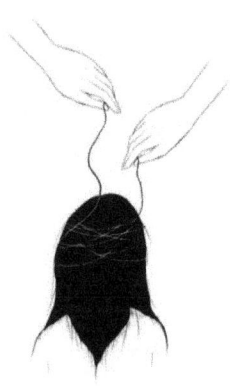

sometimes I am so weary
I wish only to fall into sleep's soft arms
lay my head on the pillow
and rest for weeks, months, years
however long it takes to soothe
the ache of constant unease in my chest
to stroke my disquieted mind
with the sweetest lullaby
that makes eyes leaden
and breath honey slow

a dreamless, quiet reverie

erin michelle

when I tell you I stared in the mirror
and saw exhaustion in my eyes
I am asking you to see the absence of myself
in the hollows of my face

please don't tell me it is not so bad

I am desperate for the rest
off a mind that stands still
that doesn't run in circles
around uncontrolled anxieties
and remains grounded
in that which is rational

I am desperate for the rest
of a body that does not shake
when met with morning each day
already distressed by
merely facing the world
one minute at a time

I am desperate for the rest
of steady breathing
where lungs remain uncrushed
able to hold a full breath
without a burning chest
and the sweet release of air

I am desperate for rest

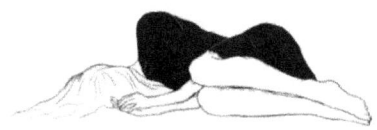

erin michelle

I am somnolent to my soul
my hands limp at my side
and heart heavy in my chest

my breaths feel sharp and jagged
the air in my lungs tainted
full of the shards of my shattered self

so tired, I wish merely to float
away from existence
into the soft arms of sleep

and the comforting dark of nothing

lay me down
let me sleep
allow spent eyes to close
and soften the breaths and sharp edges
kept at guard during days light
hum lullabies to rest unease
please, rest my unease

I am so tired

erin michelle

heavy breath midnight fears
snatching air from tight lungs
has me reaching for your warmth
an always steady hand to hold
a place to bury my fears
in the safety of your arms
where you invariably lull
my demons to a depthless sleep

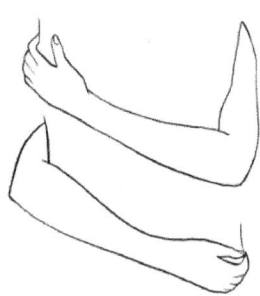

I feel empty
the hollowness only aches with the kiss of sadness
whose lips beckon sleep to shut eyes
in hopes that the nightmares stay in dark corners
allowing rest to soothe tired thoughts
sinking into the depths of quiet's cold embrace

while the demons prepare to dream

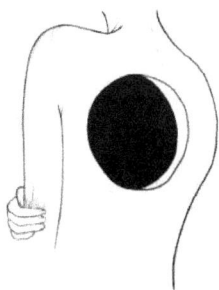

erin michelle

I don't want to be my own protagonist
and antagonist
I am tired of the constant fight
for space in my chest
for it cuts off the air when they go into battle
swords carving wounds around my heart

I am weary of the highs and lows of their story
I no longer want to house this book
I am not a bookshelf
made to hold the woes of many
for I carry enough of my own

let me rest in the pages of my own story

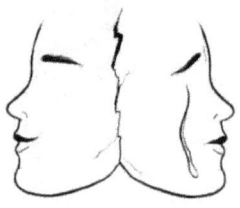

courageous conversations

it's the inability to finish my morning coffee
a slight trembling of hands
and a rambling of words

it's the desperation for sleep
with only insomnia as company
and self-doubts toying taunts

it's the weight of the world
settled heavy on my chest
and the prayer that tomorrow may be a little lighter

erin michelle

I use words like tired and exhaustion often
I am tired and exhausted often
but the words become repetitive
while the feeling thrives and twists
holding me down, tangled in sheets
bed no longer a safe haven
but a physical manifestation of my mental prison
each moment of day is a trial
leading me back to sleep
it is not a reprieve

it is my prison sentence

courageous conversations

it's a feat
to give myself the rest
I don't think I deserve
in a world where we are encouraged to burn brighter
but discards those whose light burns so bright
it flickers out

-to the lights that burnt out

LOVER

erin michelle

sleep has found me at last
for I have found safety in your arms
protection from the dark nights
that once consumed me
and my dear, you were worth each sleepless evening

each hardship I have faced you stood beside
every cracked piece of myself I laid before you
you loved and cherished
holding each bit as if it was beautiful

you are my tether to this beautiful world
when I find myself lost in my mind
your hand warm and strong in mine
my heart forever belonging to you

he is the man who speaks of my intelligence
before he ever boasts of his own
the one who kisses away tears of insecurity
with no pretense or judgement
and passionately tells me of my worth
on the days I think I've lost it

he is the first one I look for in any room
the steady hand always there to be held
the inspiration to many words
the partner to many adventures

he is the most beautiful of masculinity
he is safe, he is kind, he is home

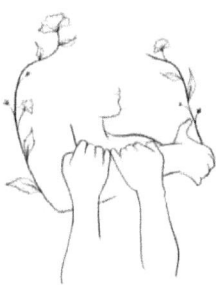

erin michelle

it is unassuming and without agenda
the way he gives love

a soft touch or word of affirmation
an acknowledgement of my successes

he is kindness and friendship
warm arms and an open heart

his strengths fill my weaknesses
as mine do his

courageous conversations

I caught him watching
as I looked at the stars
eyes alight
as though he'd discovered a new constellation
in the recesses on my mind
a new love story to be written in the sky

for now, and evermore

erin michelle

he held me so sweetly
kissed me so softly
conversed with me so deeply
and made me feel vastly

I didn't know love was given so unconditionally

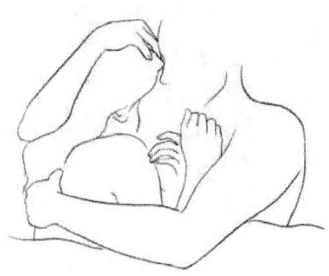

courageous conversations

he looks at me
as if I could give him the world
and I only hope I can show him a sweeter version
than the one we reside in

erin michelle

he has become my moon on clouded eve
he pierces the opaque with a kindness I still am
unsure I deserve
and his hand has never failed
to stroke love into the space
between thumb and finger
with the gentleness he knows I need
his tender smile, my world quickly
his arms my home
his laughter a refuge from the darkest nights

he showed me how to love
when I'd been taught my love was wrong
picking up the broken pieces
scattered to the wind
with patience and dedication
and placing them gently
back into the puzzle

-*thank you*

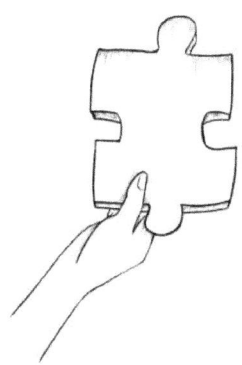

erin michelle

you taste sweeter
than any memory
any memory of your lips
could do no justice
to their sweetness upon mine

courageous conversations

3 am knows all our secrets
it knows our intimacy
both the beautiful and the harsh
it knows how your arms keep me safe
and how our bodies intertwine
it knows our quiet laughter
and our sweetest moments
it sees the late-night contemplations
and the pain we can hide in the dark
it knows the highs and lows
as it blankets us in the night

erin michelle

it's the catch of your breath
on the softest skin
between neck and collarbone
that undoes me
and the trailing kiss
to whisper in my ear
that makes me burn
but it is the adoration
in your gaze and touch

that makes me unmistakably yours

courageous conversations

I won't hide my demons from you
for this beautiful disaster belongs to you
and I have learned to trust your love
for you never saw me as damaged
only as exquisitely broken
and pieced back together
into something stronger

-kintsugi (golden joinery)

erin michelle

bitten lower lip moments
sweet hands for sinful thoughts
conversations of love between our sheets
and whispers of lust in each breathless name
each dark, hooded eye gaze
lighting me on fire
and every sugar sweet touch
marks my body with your love

let this never end

courageous conversations

he speaks my name
soft like a benediction
a sore throat gravel voice
humming to my heartstrings tune

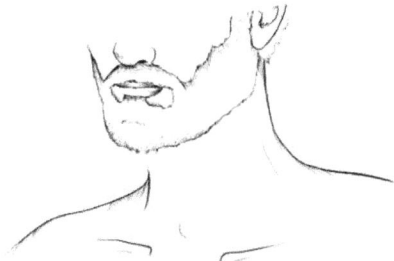

erin michelle

run soft hands to trail my spine
goosebumps follow
create patterned flesh
brush hair gently from my neck
and allow soft kisses to follow fingers
making me the storm after your calm
a calm causing calamity
as brain struggles with what body knows
what I am in these moments
that steal sweet breath
from parted lips
to give to you
for as always in these moments
I am yours

always yours

courageous conversations

I adore you, my love
I could write endless pages of our love
I could tell hundreds of stories
sing thousands of praises
look at you a million times
and still be in awe
my heart would still beat
to the sound of your cadence
skipping when you smile
thundering when your eyes burn
stopping when you tell me you love me
I could never get enough
you're the one addiction
I could never want to quit
the one song I could listen to endlessly
the path I could walk forever
I adore you, my love

erin michelle

lie with me between silk sheets
whisper sugar coated words in the dark
for they taste the sweetest from your lips
tell me about your worldly thoughts
and encourage exploration of my mind
search out my secrets and share with me yours
be mine for tonight
because morning comes too soon

he took me to the place he loved most
to share the small beauties he was raised on
to disconnect from the unnecessary
and connect once again with the soul
merely the gentle lapping of waves
as they kiss the shore for only a brief moment
as brief as the enjoyment
we search for in crowded places
when it sits before us
the untouched and pure

-inverhuron

erin michelle

he refers to me as exquisite
his voice thick with sincerity
he strokes my cheek
tracing the planes of my face
gaze intense as he memorizes each feature

and for once I believe a man when he tells me I am beautiful

what if we kissed under the willow at midnight
and whispered our desires by light of moon
what if we lay intertwined in body and mind
and dawn never came too soon
would we still be the youth or embrace our old souls
or would we merely lay until ruin
what if we kissed under the willow at midnight
sweet by the dusk of june

-what if?

erin michelle

I want to build a home with you
let our arms create the frame
and together our hands will lay this brick
we will build strong walls
so that ours may crash open with vulnerability
this will be our safehouse and dreamhouse
safe from harm and a place to dream big
we will craft memories to adorn each room
and it will be full of the light you showed me
we will fill it with love
so each room feels sweet like your kiss
and it will be ours

-our home

I breathe you in
I am a moth drawn to your flame
the circle of your arms my castle
and the softness of your lips my undoing
you undo me
to build me up again
when my insecurities berate me
I press a kiss to your neck
to feel the pulse that ignites my heart
hands grip tightly to the cotton of your shirt
I breathe you in
for you smell like sin and security
safety and sweetness
you have become my home
here I am able to just be

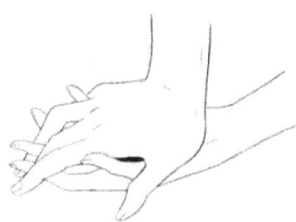

erin michelle

this stubborn heart has met its match
a match that burns as brightly as my own
not fearful of the flame
others shied away from
and you didn't run
when I drunkenly sang my love
from the floor of the shower
or when my tears flooded your shoulder
faced with demons not your own
you merely burned brighter
lighting my way through the dark
and slowly your flame has become my
enlightenment
to a world I was once so jaded by

courageous conversations

he painted his lips to mine
in a color so vibrant
lavender bloomed on my tongue
and we spoke only through the press
of paint tendered to skin
and the shared breath of botanicals
as addictive as rosemary sweet gin
that inspired the art on my lower lip
brushed by his bite
that leaves me whispering his name
like a grace
good graces be this artform
of brushes, strokes, and flowers

erin michelle

I fell into you
into the words that you crafted
and the actions you upheld
into the eyes reflecting forested skies
I fell into your being
the kindness you sprinkle
like soft summer rain
and the strength you embody
in character and mind
I fell so far into you
for your intelligence is as intoxicating
as your lips on my skin
and each moment with you feels beautiful

I didn't know the world could be so beautiful

so, I fell into you
I've fallen for you
I am falling
but it feels like flying

we fall in love over and over
not a one-time romance
but a continuous courting
so dance me across the living room
and kiss me for the first time again
and let our glances last just a little too long
and our touches a little too brief
let us make love sweetly and with laughter
as we explore one another all over again
let's flirt in the mornings
or afternoons or evenings
and go on big and small adventures
so we never tire of escapades together
let's watch stars, eat fine food, sing in the car
and laugh till our bellies hurt
let's love softer and harder
ferocious yet gentle
frantically but slowly

let's fall in love everyday

ANGST

erin michelle

existing is rawer than I expected
for one does not merely exist
we thrash in discontent
we fall hard, scraping knees
with no one to offer us a band aid

we fuck to feel something other than pain
and make love to remind us of the softer things
we raise new bread earners
not telling them capitalism cares nothing for them
and struggle to understand
why our world is still so broken and unjust

to exist is to live in conflict
it is to give away pieces of yourself
to meet the demand of existence
to sell your soul to society for a penny in return
and only find reassurance
in likes on a self-edited photo
we share skin like currency
yet hide emotions that may present us as weak
we are merely the contents of a social media grid
we exist to please
yet find no pleasure in ourselves
behind locked doors

doors locked
candle doused
lights dimmed
check again
and again
and again
let the paranoia rule
let it dictate each action
fear the worse
check again
and again
and again
till eve becomes dawn
and sleep never said hello
are the doors locked?
the candles doused?
the lights dimmed?

can I even remember to breathe?

erin michelle

my heart sits in my throat
fluttering erratically
beating out of time
pulsing with unease
my unease
to this broken world
with so much beauty
wrongly condemned

it is bubbling under the surface
continually harder to keep at bay
please, give me a little longer
let me keep my peace for one more moment
choke it back like bile in my throat
yet still it simmers
the anxiety awakening
stretching languidly across my body
the depression creating a clouded cover
a rainy day for the beast beneath my skin

today I will struggle

erin michelle

I ache with the fullness of the emotions
I have allowed no space
for they have swelled and flowed
from toes to fingertips
demanding to be given room and reflection
their ebb and flow now a raging current
an undertow sweeping me away
water filling lungs, forcing me to adapt or drown
learning to find oxygen in each wave
less leaving this world
and I have learned I must follow each ebb and flow
with due diligence and perspective
so I am not lost in this current forever

-sit with your discomfort

courageous conversations

vulnerability does not come easy
to my uncompromising will
it does not sit gently in the candlelight
it burns hot with the flame
even when tears singe the light

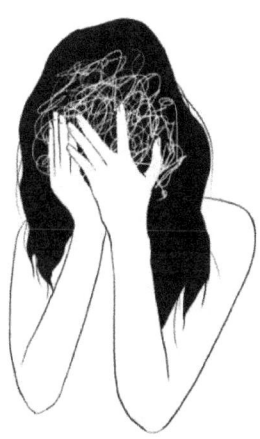

erin michelle

what age was I
when I lost my youth
where did it fall
beneath the cracks
how do I find it once again

I miss innocence

courageous conversations

my unrest breed's displeasure
frustration of that which I hold no control
irritation runs rampant
parading through my mind
each item of discontent
a catalogue of my indignation
in the pages of my thoughts
one I flip through all too often
and no, I hold you no ill will
I am sorry you fear my crossfire
you are too close to the sadness and anger
for it holds hands with love and lust
as do all the intense emotions I feel
I struggle to discern them
when my mind won't stop yelling
when I feel the world is shouting
for me to do better
and no, it's not you
you never shout
your soul is too kind and gentle
the tranquility to my chaos
but that too brings me vexation

erin michelle

keep moving
stay busy
don't stop
more fiddling
anxious twitch
don't let it catch you
keep running
the buzzing getting closer
forget what you were doing
move faster, fiddle more
it is here, you are caught
find a dark corner
and curl up against the attack

-anxiety attack

I've been trapped in my own cage
of hazy sight and a blanketed mind
locked in a fight for the blissful numbness
accompanied by aching lungs
and suppressed suffering
for I am unsure I will survive
the world outside my cage

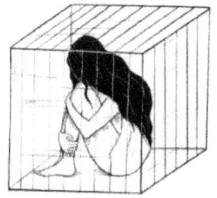

erin michelle

I can't get my words on a page
they sit in my stomach
heavy on my heart
fester under my skin

I watch them scrawl across my mind
desperate for the release of ink
angry with the confine they are locked in
screaming to be written

I agonize over the thought
of bringing children into this world
for I fear what they will endure
after inheriting the features
that caused me many tears in the mirror
and late-night idealization of what might be
if I was only a little thinner, a little prettier
slightly quieter or even just a touch smarter
I wish no child to feel such self-doubt
as I do in my own skin

erin michelle

I have carefully crafted each piece of this armour
a steely gaze and distinguished stature
the only clue of the walls I've constructed

I am always ready for battle

my worrying leads to pacing
worry.
pace.
worry.
pace.
worry.
pace.
worrying crescents from nails in palm
pacing till the path of my anxiety
is shaped clearly in the carpet
of my sparse and shabby apartment
worry and pace

erin michelle

my thoughts jump like stones on the water
rippling in directions unknown
disturbing peaceful serenity
with the agitation of my anxiety

courageous conversations

I am honeyed glass thoughts
sweet, yet sharp to swallow
cutting gentle throats
inhaling blood and honey
sticky sweet to make the pain abate
still, each gulp is sharper
choking on rivulets of words
this is what it is to drown
in my own mind

erin michelle

my soul feeds this pen
aching my hand to write when it's too full
seeking release from the emotions it's consumed
no longer able to digest the reel of my mind
so, I write until this pen has no ink
because I am so full it hurts
and I wish to be starved of this pain

slow violence
lilting with menacing beauty
the cruelest mistress
though the one that satisfies
her deviled tongue
still coated in sugar
she's an ode to
hurts so good

-anxiety: the cruel mistress

erin michelle

it seethes under the surface
violent and lethal; parasitic and predatory
I bet you can see it sometimes
it is the dark crescents beneath my eyes
it is the shaking in my limbs
it is the agitation in which I speak
for while I speak, it screams
screams and claws and cackles and cuts
and it is never sated
I am lucky to make it through the day
before it pushes tears from my eyes
and bile from my throat
as it slowly strips me away
from the inside out

courageous conversations

I am full of words
brimming with sentences unspoken
expressions yet to meet paper
and poems yet to be crafted
and so many words
are lost in the fray
so much so, I wish to fall
into the dark corners
of my mind's library
to pluck each lost word
from dusty shelves
and arrange them
into the greatest novel

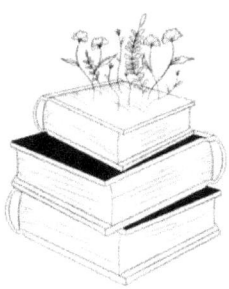

erin michelle

I'm not sure I even know
what it is to breathe with ease
my chest always heavy
air dry, lungs cracked
fear heavy on my mind
a devil on each shoulder
for I don't believe there are angels left

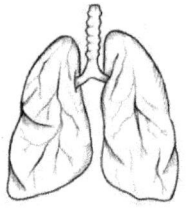

courageous conversations

giving words to anxiety
is like trying to breath underwater
hopeless to understand
until you are the one drowning

ILLUMINATIONS

erin michelle

our world is so beautifully broken
daily media showing us the bad
yet I strive to see the good
in the hands that were held out to me
at my darkest hours
the laughter in my friends faces
despite the isolation we live in
the constant fight of our youth
to leave this world better than we found it
and the comfort I find in my parents
regardless of the illnesses faced
for it cannot be all bad
I refuse to see only the bad
in a world that creates such beautiful
things, people, and memories

courageous conversations

I am inspired by each poet before me
the breath of their emotion
the power of the spaces between
every chosen word
each expression of wonder, lust, elation, rage
crafted into something of beauty and power
a beacon for the soft-spoken individuals
looking for someone to tell them they are not alone

-you are not alone

erin michelle

I woke up lighter today
felt I was in my own body once more
could see with a new clarity

for the sun was a little brighter
the snow a bit crisper
my face less shadowed

my shaking had ceased
I breathed evenly again
and I laughed for the first time in a very long time

-is this what it is to feel happy?

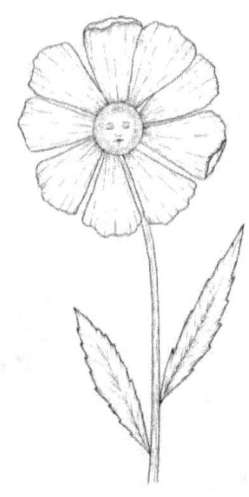

courageous conversations

I found a kindred spirit
between words and art
where creativity soothed
our dulling aches and pains
as we shared tears
over lessons, hardships, and the little things
to create something beautiful
that may comfort others
who too have felt lost in their own sentiment

-to my artist

erin michelle

I watched magic in a jazz club
between old radio rasp and a trumpets croon
music weaving goosebumps over my skin
as each improvised bar brought forth new beauty
each note an old friend, yet a new sound
with classics dispersed in between
and I was taken over the rainbow
with four notes and the love of the music

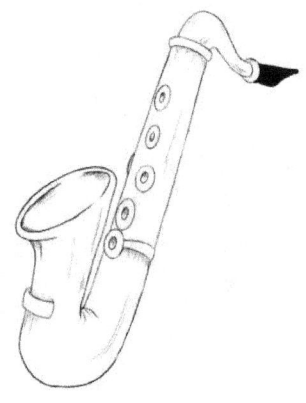

make space for your pain
welcome it with kind arms
and show it the gentle love needed
become friends with suffering
share thoughts and tears
learn to love the hurt
and that love will be returned
with a tenderness only pain can give

-we will heal together

erin michelle

a hollowed shell
gently picked from sea foamed water
softly held, touched, treasured
by the little hazel eyed girl
until it was no longer hollow
for it housed her sweet affections

-*childhood*

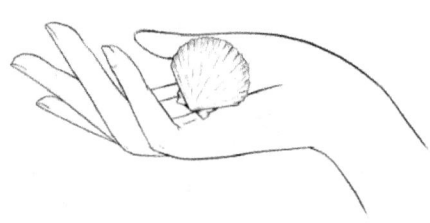

the most stunning gift
between the pages of Joni Mitchell
was finding the pieces
of whom I want to become

a broken artist with a full heart and endless words

-morning glory on the vine by Joni Mitchell

erin michelle

I laughed so hard today my cheeks hurt
and I touched them in wonder
what beauty it is to smile
with the lightness of laughter
and unhindered joy
cleared from the dark
sweeping dust and despair away
if only for a moment

I live for these moments

courageous conversations

brick blockade neighbourhood
art streaked by midnight vagabonds
to scorn the judgers
and inspire the enlightened

morning coffee cools as conversations animate
window watchers observe passerby's
newspapers folded, shaken, and folded again
the sounds of a morning melody

preparing the crowds for survival
caffeinated and fearless

erin michelle

I cry for harmonies heartbreaking sigh
to melodies mournful ballad
crescendoing to a precipice
where my tears fall unabashed
chest heaving with grief
conveyed from the simplicity
of ivory keys

only the broken wade in poetic verses
and find the wholeness in the scattered sentences
where hope was lost but words persisted

-for the broken

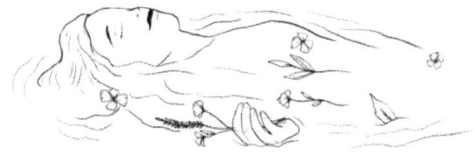

erin michelle

she wishes to only see the beautiful things
lost so they may be to those passing by
whom trample the wildflowers
growing through cracks in sidewalks
lost in thoughtless thinking

yet she lingers
placing dandelions in her hair
secret smiles to herself
she admires those in love
embraces a deep breath of wintered pine
basks in the sigh of sunrise

little does she know
she is the sweetest beauty of them all

to the women who have come before me
and the ones who will come after
to those who paved the way
and made sure we were defined
by our strength and intelligence
and not our smiles and curves
to those who fought to cast a ballot
and those who said no to status quo
placing themselves in the line of fire
and refusing to move
to those who proved a woman could manage
more than just a household
and fought for the right to be seen as an equal
and a force to be reckoned with
going toe to toe with misogyny
and emerging triumphant
to my mother, my aunts, my soul sisters, and the
women I look up to

thank you for ensuring I know my worth
and never accept less than what I deserve

-international women's day

erin michelle

I am content in this home of love
with its early morning coffee chats
and reflections of happiness in the hardships
I am grateful for this opportunity
to laugh with my mother and father
to enjoy their company
beyond parental duty towards friendship
and to continue learning
what makes them unique
for they embody the kindness I aspire to give
the determination I desire to reach my success
and the love I wish to pass to my children

and I cannot adequately express my gratitude
that they are mine

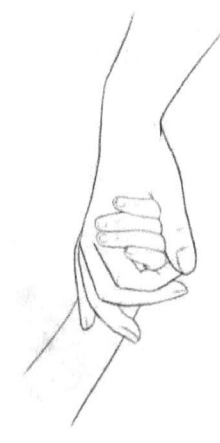

courageous conversations

ask me for a secret and I'll tell you a revelation
one I have kept hidden in pockets and corners
and the cobwebbed shelves of my thoughts
it may not be the answer you sought
but it was the one I found

*I did not think I would make it to today
so, tomorrow I will start living*

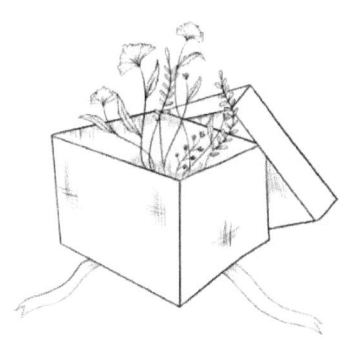

erin michelle

I just want to write
get words onto a page
and feel each letter
as it is crafted from a piece of my soul
I want to bleed my mind
into each sentence
watching as the broken becomes beautiful
and my tired mind eases
I want to share what it is like
to persevere through mind's trials
and walk out with battle scars on the other side
marking victory

I want you to know what it is to triumph over your demons

courageous conversations

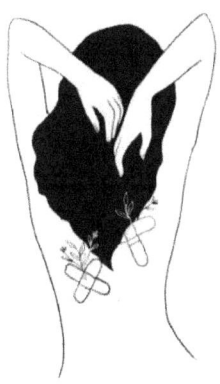

erin michelle

I found it for a brief moment today
in between the quiet lulls and loud noise
just a split second
minute, yet so full of power
so precious I held it gently
cupped in shaking palms
and it was beautiful
it spoke to a future yet to come
perhaps even an end to the trials

for it was hope
fragile, yet prominent and strong
that I held in my hands
that had weathered many storms
and still endured
it was the love and laughter
I was sure was lost along the way
it was home, sweet, and warm
it was happiness

and most importantly, it was mine

DESPONDENT

courageous conversations

who am I when no one is in the room
when the candlelight fades
and I am left with my contemplations

am I still the girl who once partook in revelry
whose laughter came easy
offering smiles to all around

or am I the one sitting here alone
whose heart aches with pain
and eyes flooded
from cruel words sung by internal demons

or does it even matter
who I am, how I feel, what I see
when no one seems troubled enough to know

-*am I even real?*

erin michelle

my feelings seem too much
for this vessel of flesh, blood, and bone
seem so much greater
than the weight this body can carry
I must have been crafted wrong
for how am I to ever
endure such a burden
as the one I carry in my mind

I'm trying to love this body
this form I was gifted
but the mirror is yelling insults
and my brain is whispering lies
and I can't help resenting
this not so perfect figure
the little too curvy, too big, too tall, too not societal standard body
that holds the most important things
courage, strength, humour, kindness
but I can't get past the cover of my book

why can't I love myself?

erin michelle

my body is in agony
wracked with the pain
of unrelenting emotional duress

every breath too sharp
each movement unsteady
and filled with discomfort

sleep lies on the wrong side of the bed
and my eyes lie dull
shadows dark beneath

the tears fall often
provoked and not
shaking bones with weary sobs

I am in pain that none can see
my silent suffering
still a stigma to this world

-depression

I like to dwell in my melancholy some nights
although I know I could force a smile

for sometimes the dark is easier to see in than day

erin michelle

I hurt today
even in the most beautiful of places
an awkwardness in my skin
that I can't place a finger on
just a quiet persistent unease
that brings sadness to the lovely of my mind
coaxing silence from my lips
and stiffness from my hands
even as those closest urge me to smile

my prayers come in the shape of little white pills
swallowed to keep the demons at bay
and they rattle in the bottle
an audible reminder of my desire to find quiet
my daily fix of normalcy
small in my hand
yet heavy from the weight
of mental oppression carried

maybe today will be peaceful

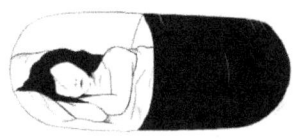

erin michelle

I don't ebb and flow
like those who easily exist
I crash and disrupt
like roaring river rapids
a never-ending collision
of thoughts and action
slowly wearing me down
pebbles on the riverbed
sinking and drowning
crashing and disrupting

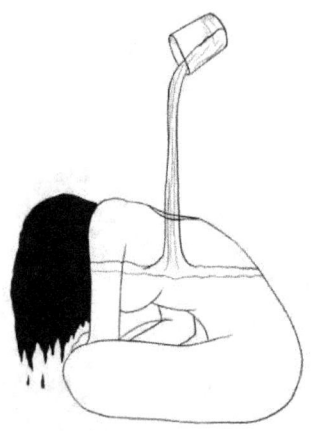

courageous conversations

"help me, I am lost"
I whisper to myself
I no longer know which way to turn
in the labyrinth of my mind
how to outrun my thoughts
and the jarring pain that follows
I have not eaten in hours, days, weeks?
I no longer recall
and I am parched from the tears shed
I am aching from muscles unused
I am too tired to run anymore

"help me, I am lost"

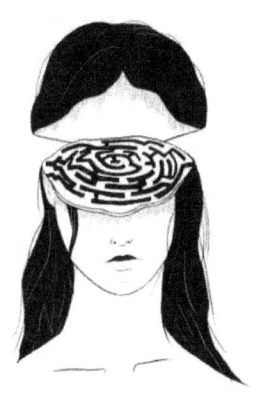

erin michelle

some days it is too difficult to put pen to paper
I am fearful of what the ink may say
ashamed of my own darkness
tired of the fight, ready to give up

those are words I don't wish to share
for they frighten even me
when they scream in my head
reminding me of my proclivity to the night

the night with no moon no stars and no hope

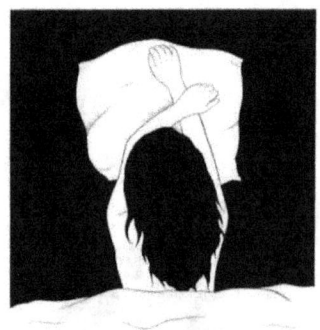

courageous conversations

I broke last week
choking on lungs full of smoke
a reprieve from my mind's bickering
neglecting my body in anger
for what it fails to be

erin michelle

she is a chemically romanced high
a lighthouse without luminescence
dancing with the imbalance
of fighting swords in her mind

tired of the useless noise
perpetrating her unease
so back into the arms of
a lover's drug tipped embrace

-addiction

it is a bad day today
I am searching for strength
buried deep beneath exhaustion
I have been clawing all morning
handfuls of dirt piling beside me
"one more handful," I tell myself
I know I left it here somewhere
my nails have cracked
and my hands bleed

please tell me I am getting close

erin michelle

I've carried this incumbrance too long
suffering under the affliction
of the storm in my mind
as it rains and rains and rains
as if to drown me in my own tears
and yell thunderously in my head
of each of my shortcomings
each crack like a whip to my skin
every lightning bolt a burnout for my mind
and I cannot see the end of this madness

courageous conversations

I have not written in months
for I fear of the words that will reach this page
the thoughts that have been screaming in my head
the expressions of self-loathing
that pit self against self
and have me crawling into bed at 2 pm
in an effort to shut out the world
these are not the pretty words
not the shiny words
not the happy words
they are the words whispered
in the back of my head
pushing and clawing their way into every corner
until it is all I can hear
until I no longer want to hear, or see, or think, or be

erin michelle

it's the sweetness in satisfaction
licked with the original flame of sin
a soft burn in all the right places
battered and bruised kind of love

the one you know to query
to fear both bark and bite
but the pain is illicit, delectably so
making this flame dangerous

for it is that of the deadliest fire
that turns fists to caresses
screams into sighs
and perpetuates the addicting abuse

-abusive infatuation

courageous conversations

I wish the wings of the butterfly to remain untouched
to stay pristine, to remain innocent and pure
to fly with ease and beauty
for my wings were blackened
with truths of cruelty
and loss of childhood ignorance
and the touch of dirty hands

erin michelle

hand me the first aid kit
in the left drawer under the sink
so I can begin to patch this wound
for it has festered and weeps with sentimentality
the finest feelings blade sharp
flaying protective layers of skin and mirth
that hid the commiseration that now drips on tile
crimson stark against marble
I thought I could hide it so well
until you found me here on the bathroom floor

courageous conversations

I lived in my depression today
letting my fight cease
for the numbness to take root
for care to fade into dark
and emptiness to fill
the spaces in all my cracks
I let the sharp edges cut
and the hope to become despair
for it is easier some days
to give into the fight

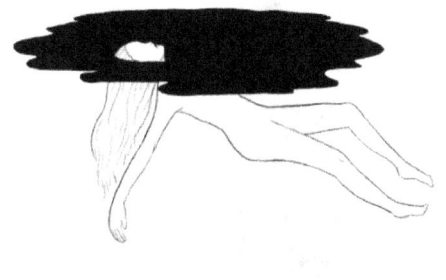

erin michelle

depollute me of the tar
that drips from tear-stained eyes
streaks of black my armour
of the battle I wage within
draw away this toxicity
that resides in my waking and resting moments
for I have found nowhere safe to hide
so I face it and face it and face it again
I will not quake in its shadows
I will reach into its blackness
and pull from it the heart it has stolen from me

and we shall do war

I live with this affliction
so others may not suffer
so others know they are not alone
so others read my words and understand
that the world which has beaten them down
will also hold them up
that hundreds, thousands, millions stand with them
that their agony is worth living through

I live with this affliction
so I have a purpose to this pain

erin michelle

let me write this desolate melody
to be played by symphonies in my memory
for woe can be oh so beautiful

make the audience cry with my story
show them the minor chords crafting depression
and the angst that steals their breath

hold the last note just a little longer
to show them I tried to hold on
for the beauty that was my life

let everyone sit in the deafening silence of that chord
and understand a little better
the battle of the mentally afflicted

-for all those lost to suicide

REFLECTIONS

enlighten me to the world
my fears wish to conceal
search out the identity
I left discarded in the field
where I lost the battle of wills
unlay it from its rest
and help me sew the frayed ends
to my tattered soul
breathe warm air
on my frigid lips
and thaw the coldness
I wrapped around my heart
be my shelter
while I endure the storm I tried to numb
allow my tears to create a downpour
that results in the grace of acceptance
and show me the kindness
I have not learned to give to myself

erin michelle

I don't live in the soft world anymore
I ache with the broken
piled carelessly in the corner
no longer played with

I am sharp as the scalpel
that drew patterned lace on my skin
and deadly as a siren's song
that called sailors to the depths

I shatter like the lightning
that fractures from the skies
and roar like the thunder
who must scream to be heard

I feel with the magnitude of crashing plates
remaking earth in their anger
yet am silent
as I sit with the chaos

clearness of mind
is not the clarity for which I hoped
black and white is fiction in a grey world
acting as canvas for prisms to bleed colour on
till my eyes beg for respite
from the emotions I've cowered from

erin michelle

I wasn't there to protect you
and it has suppressed me in my guilt
my mourning for our youth
but I am here now for the little girl we were
I am here when he yells
and places hands where you wish they were not
I am here to wipe the tears his threats left
and to prop you tall when you stand to leave
I am here for your healing
and will remain strong when the trauma unearths
and we will grow in the tilled ground
into something that little girl would find beautiful and
strong

courageous conversations

I thought I'd lost it
amidst the newscaster's coffee report and the protests
for the right just to be
maybe it was stolen by
the chaotic political agenda and the illness deemed
less important than the polls
I feared it had fallen between the cracks
of police enforcement and police brutality
or perhaps it had laid beneath
the inequitably judged and the wrongly lost

its lack of presence ached
like rocks sitting on my chest
lost without the ability
to change what beheld this world

until I was reminded by the fiery anger
forged in the feelings of helplessness
that they could not take
my ability to make a difference
my words were my power
my echo my war drum
my voice my greatest weapon
my action my greatest gift

erin michelle

I have lost myself a thousand times over
yet only found myself a few
the astray versions still wander
frankly, so do the found
and perhaps I am just a wanderer
forever searching for that which can't be found
but I keep falling into myself
so deeply
I cannot crawl back through the rabbit hole
instead stuck in my reflections
is this what alice felt in wonderland?
am I one of the lost boys?
is each childhood movie trying to tell me
I've gone mad?
will I find a way home in this dark maze?
is there meaning to any of this?
I have so many questions
a growing list that is so heavy
I have to try to choke it down
yet it falls from my tongue
and people say I ramble too much
but I am merely searching for answers
and lost versions of myself
even my cup of coffee
now a reflection pool of scrutiny
did I always love to hate the silence?
will this pain become more manageable?
why is this coffee no longer hot?
where did today go?

I am falling again

a broken cup chipped
hot coffee morning
tangled hair accompanied
by clear thought
a lyricist with a song
to the tulip with the sun
a path not found
but mine, nonetheless

erin michelle

today I feel everything
from the melancholy blue of my walls
to the satin of my shirt that slips from my shoulder
soft as fingertips tracing patterns of collarbones
and harsh as songs that broke hearts
with nothing more than words placed
in an order to convey anguish of mind

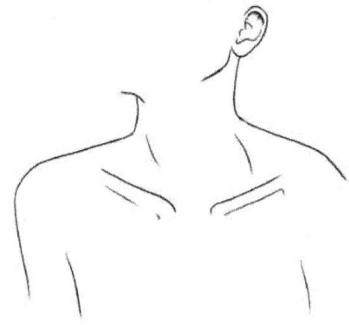

he calls me his beautiful disaster
unintentional cruelty in bright eyes blue
a horrific beauty in reshaped skin and sharper wit
ever so slightly too acute
as such, unable to be treasured
for the uniqueness possessed

erin michelle

I masticated a piece of the sky
chewing and swallowing the thickness of night
viscous like nectar in my throat
coating my voice in constellations
so I may speak stars into the universe
hum celestial beings into existence
whisper cosmos in your ear
and craft art in the interstellar

oh my star
in a blue moon sky
constellation eyes
and a dreamer's gaze

erin michelle

how to write a poem...

break.

so thoroughly you shatter like glass
try and collect the shards
let the blood from cut palms mix with salty tears
let it spill onto the glass's reflection
and pause
suffer, observe, endure
then write the slivers back together
bind them in gold
and adorn them in jewels
draw readers in with its beauty
but never hide
the blood and tears that built words
that made somebody feel
beyond that what is beautiful
and broke you

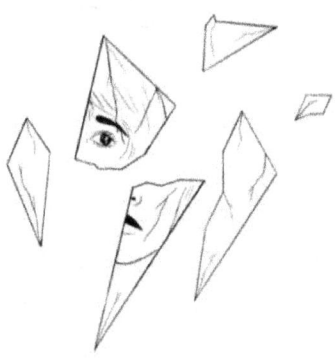

I want to be done this chapter
of sleeping pills and hazy eyes
unshed tears on the precipice of glassy gazes
throbbing heads compensation for sweet thoughts
and the ache of sleeps romantic nothings

quench soft sore throats, with sugar-coated words
to forge strong chords
grounding lilting harmonies to steadfast melody
end the bar; close the book

start a new chapter

tonight, I'm lost in trails of thoughts
paths through canopied woods
equal parts sinister and breathtaking
a chilling fairy tale of struggle and strife

where the path less followed
is heavily overgrown yet full of enchantment
wonders and tales of joy
a blissful reverie I had forgotten

a path I wish to take once more

day is easy
soft with the suns kiss
fresh, full of breath and freedom
yet night is harsh
even amongst moon and candles glow
shadowed panes cast sharp edges

I am eve
lingering between soft and sharp, day and night
round cheeks cut by dark curtains of hair
fresh air in the shadows
moons breath in darkness's freedom
lost between light and black

starlight perhaps

erin michelle

I am the dark shadow that dances with fires flame
who feels with the tenacity of a wildfire
and moves with the grace of the burn
I am harsh like the kiss of the flame
that entices you to feel its bite
lulled into security by the embers that glow
smouldered gaze and the sultry flicker of a smile
brings you to the kindles edge
as you step into the blaze
bound by my dark shadows
welcome home darling

courageous conversations

storms sooth the chaos in my chest
perhaps it is because we speak the same language
of thunderous roars and raindrop whispers
cracking with the same passion
as lightning fractured skies
we are kin, ferocious yet soft
bringing forth showers of calm with powerful words

erin michelle

I gaze upon her often
the strong nose, almond eyes, chocolate hair
she should be so familiar
she should be home
she should be me

yet I am an imposter in the mirror

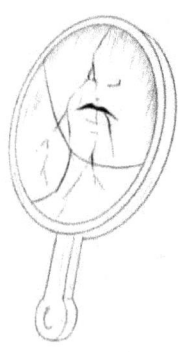

courageous conversations

I have been waging a war against my body
with unkind words and perfectionist expectations
I am crueler than any outsider would be
I cut deep with reckless abandon
and berate that which gives me life
I am the greatest enemy to myself
shedding tears for that which should be celebrated
weighing my figure over the value of my mind
choosing vanity over my worth
I am tired of this battle
it is time to find peace

-*self-love*

odd curiosity
was the woman who stood in the mirror
running hands over curves she was always unkind to
trying to show her love in some manner
for the body that got her through many trials
who now walked proudly saying look at me
look at my strength
look at my beauty
look at my power

I am sorry for running before we could walk
I was so busy fleeing I forgot how to slow down
how to live with you on my back
how to get stronger with your weight
how to give you space in my mind
and learn to live together

-dear mental illness

erin michelle

december breath through painted lips sigh
this is where the mentally afflicted dream
nightmares fueled by a melatonin high
fingernails sharp palms crescent seams

welcome home kin to the brokens' eve
sharp yet soft is the night we embody
art is in the eye in which does perceive
as we bend, almost break in mind and body

let our souls be lines that draw fine art
to bleed us of our continuous pain
for we shall continue to impart
art inspired by midnight's strange domain

we are the artist, the paint, the brush
december air drawing cheeks flush

swipe a tear from my cheek and bring it to your lips
for emotions are sweetest when raw
"never apologize for the depth you feel"
"it is beautiful, your passion is beautiful"

hold my face in your hands
and kiss the tears as they fall
show me my sentience is not weakness
show me these broken bits can be whole
be the ribbon that wraps the pieces together

fill each fissure with something saccharine
to balance the bitter in my chest
and remove the sharpness of each breath

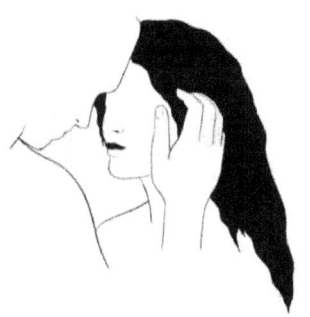

erin michelle

she is kissed by fire
marked by raised skin
from the flames that couldn't deny her
a whimsical beauty dangerous as sin

from a tortuous caress of fiery lips

her eyes burn gold
alight with the unnerving intelligence
that allow her words to burn tenfold
and sooth with warm eloquence

she leaves trails of ash
a phoenix; fiery and fierce
until she passes in burst of light
to be reborn once again, in the heart of the willing

disarm intrusive thoughts
don your armour and fight
for your demons thrive on your fear
show them no weakness
purge fear from your mind
and remove anxieties control
you, my dear, are a fighter
you are armed with the weapons you need
you are strength and steel
willful and weaponized
and you will be victorious

erin michelle

lavender sighs
lost thoughts wander
in candle laden rooms
tear-stained pillows
disarray of sheets

lavender sighs
ink smeared hands
hold beautifully painful words
a lonely poet
a broken woman

yet, her lavender sighs
craft words; yield words
her power is
the lovely arrangement of words
dipped in lavender sighs

cleanse my soul of the thoughts unspoken
gently wipe away the layers of disgust
I've placed on my inner beauty
remind me of my love for myself
remind me I am allowed to love myself
remind me to leave tears shed
and sleepless nights in the wind to dry
as I wash them from my skin
scrub away the dirt of my dangerous words
expressions of my lack of ability
and perceived failures
thoughts meant to cause unnecessary pain
remind me once more of happiness

erin michelle

this book is coming to a close
I've spilled my thoughts
for your eyes to admire
and your soul to feel
we've found pain in these words
and solace in these pages
each sentiment worth more to me
than anyone could ever offer
and I hope they will mean something to you
that you will earmark the pages
that made you feel
and wear out these verses
till the spine is worn
if you cry, let the pages hold your sentience
and if your heart soars
hold the pages closer
if you feel alone
remember we walked this story together
and never forget to keep having

Courageous Conversations

erin michelle

with love,
erin michelle

ABOUT THE AUTHOR

Erin grew up in Calgary, Alberta and is now a Master's student at the University of Ottawa studying Environmental Sustainability. She was diagnosed with anxiety and depression in 2016 and has continued to advocate for the mental health community ever since. Her debut poetry collection, 'show me your scars' was her introduction into the poetic discussion of mental health and 'courageous conversations' continues that. When she isn't writing, she can be found hiking, drinking copious amounts of coffee, travelling, and baking!

Follow for more poetry
www.erinmichellepoetry.com
@erinmichellepoetry

erin michelle

ABOUT THE ARTIST

Emily grew up on the countryside of Calgary Alberta. She loves art, flowers, woodland creatures, film photography, and the way that the tops of acorns look like tiny hats. Emily is inspired by the beauty of nature, and she often incorporates these themes into her artwork. When she's not drawing, she can be found drinking tea or petting dogs.

Follow for more recent works
@emmiejoyart

www.ingramcontent.com/pod-product-compliance
Lightning Source LLC
Chambersburg PA
CBHW050237120526
44590CB00016B/2122